Growing Up Lawton

"Ridgewood"

The Greatest Community As I Know It

1949-2000s

Estelle Trapp Young

Copyright © 2023
Estelle T. Young

All Rights Reserved

No portion of this publication may be reproduced, stored in any electronic system or transmitted in any form or by any means, electronic, mechanical, photocopy, recording, or otherwise, without written permission from the author.

ISBN: 9798336025156

Imprint: Independently published

All scriptures were quotes from the King James Version (KJV) Bible in the Public Domain.

The cover design is a family picture provided by the author.

Printed in the United States of America.

Dedication and Acknowledgements

This book is dedicated to my family:
My deceased parents are Henry Trapp and Leila Howard Trapp. My deceased siblings are Ollie, Almeta, Beatrice, Mary Ella, Leila Mae, Carolyn, James, Charles, and Louis. My deceased sister-in-law is Irene.

My only living sibling, William Trapp.

To Quintus Leon Young, my son, Verdell (the greatest daughter-in-law), and Minister Priscilla Pelzer (my niece I raised).

To my grands Quintus II, Justin, Little Estelle (Velica Estelle) Yvonne. Three Great Grands: Jamari, Solomon, and Jeremiah.

To all my nieces and nephews.

The Davis Children, Taylor Children, Trapp Children, Jackson Children, Boyles Children, My special nieces and nephews Mary Ann and Ronald. Alma and Stan, Ronald (who has always called me his brown sugar), and Linda, My sister-in-law Minister Charlene Trapp,

Moniet, and (Lil) Louis. Shanna, Molly, Karen and Eddie, Bertha and Bubby, my main man Tra, and (Lil) Leila. To my son by another mother, Deputy Chief Melron Kelly, and family.

To Norman Caldwell, who has been an integral part of my life, and his daughters Leah and Cinese.
To all the families on Lawton and Ridgeway Streets: The Macks, Watkins, Spanns, Lawhorns, Johnsons, Belton families, Bethels, Elkins, Johnsons, Geters, Reese's, Hills, Lyles, Pearsons, Gates, Salters, Hollis, Youngs, Davises, Robinson, Goodwins, Martins, Tidwell, and Tuckers. All these families had a significant impact on my life in a positive way.

The Ridgewood Baptist Church Family. My friends Ida Tyler, Althea Porterfield, Carrie Lyles, Jannie Nelson, and my computer fixer Faith Williams. Mary Elkins, a friend for life, talked about our careers and what we would do as adults.

A very special thanks to my deceased friend, who taught me and many other children in the community a lot about school before ever attending, Doctor Catherine Spann Davoll. A teacher at heart, she was before ever attending college and becoming an educator.

To my deceased childhood friends, Lizzie Mack,

Barbara Ann Watkins, Vivian Lawhorne Hill, and Catherine Tucker Gholson, who played and shared many happy days growing up together and sharing many secrets.

To Dr. Ezell Pittman, who said over and over again, write the book.

Table of Contents

Dedication and Acknowledgements

Foreword i

Introduction iii

Chapter 1

   The Community 1

Chapter 2

   Families of the Community 5

Chapter 3

   The Layout of the House 7

Chapter 4

   The Outside Toilets 11

Chapter 5

   How We Survived 14

Chapter 6

   The Big Move, "Those that can do, those that can't, watch." 19

Chapter 7

   Families Helping Families 23

Chapter 8

   Nicknames 31

Chapter 9

   The Porch School 34

Chapter 10
> Neighborhood Protection 37

Chapter 11
> Neighborhood Entertainment 40

Chapter 12
> The Neighborhood Stores and Entrepreneurs 49

Chapter 13
> The Church 51

Chapter 14
> The School 55

Chapter 15
> The Community Stores and Other Services 58

Chapter 16
> The Caddies and Golfers 75

Chapter 17
> Moving ON 77

Chapter 18
> Community Icons 79

About The Author 81

Foreword

At first glance, we see just two ladies sitting on the porch. What we don't see is that they lived across the street from each other for decades. They were two of the greatest women on this side of heaven. Any day, you could go to either of their homes and be welcomed with open arms of acceptance and good food. Any day, but always on Sunday, both their homes were open to feed whoever stopped by. A trail of cars followed them as they, most of the time, walked home from Ridgewood Church.

These ladies quietly influenced the lives of hundreds of people. At the same time, they took the time to pour wisdom, knowledge, and understanding into our minds and hearts. This was a twenty-four-seven operation that we really didn't realize at the time. It was not until I was an adult that I realized what they had done, and how they had been such a renowned influence on my life through the act of their "constant pouring".

They poured into us as they talked, and they listened, fed, touched, laughed, corrected, instructed, and shared their experiences: all these things in so many ways and so many days; they poured, and they poured. They poured into us whenever we were in their presence, and the pitcher they poured from was never empty. They were somehow never empty. They always had something to pour into us, even if it was through a chore they gave us to do.

My prayer is that we are or that we become "Pourers" to honor these great women and what they poured into us and continue the legacy of Lawton Street.

Gale Johnson-Montgomery, MBA
"Live On Purpose"

Introduction

The scriptures say, "Write the vision and make it plain." As I write this book, I have to reflect on the principles of God's word and how it has kept me over the years. As I ponder how I grew up, I know that God was also in my life and was always there for me when I made mistakes and when I did what was right and pleasing in his sight.

There are many things that I have learned in life, but two of them stay with me daily. Listen to the first mind that speaks to you because that is the holy spirit giving you guidance. Listen to the first mind, and you won't go wrong. The other thing that I remember daily is *sit down, don't tell you to get up*. Do something daily and stay active. Teenagers do not seem to have a sense of caring and have lost all respect for their parents, seniors, and peers. How can we help them to get back to family values and face reality?

When we lost the sense of caring for our children and the younger people, changing the way that the new generation raised their children, we lost the village. As I see it, until we start raising our children as we were raised, and our children see us as parents and not their friends, things are going to remain the same or get worse. As we were growing up, the older people in the neighborhood would always say, "Never forget where you come from." Always treat people like you want to be treated, and trust the Lord.

Growing up in Ridgewood, as I knew it, as young people, we were all exposed to the church. It didn't matter what you had on; when Sunday came, you went to Sunday school, Morning Service, Baptist Training Union, and every child in the neighborhood had to do something. Sometimes, you might be in church all day. Many children today in our community don't go to church and, in so many neighborhoods, have never been to church. I think this is the training ground for respect and getting to know who God is. Children in the neighborhood knew they had to respect all their elders. It didn't matter what happened on the weekend. Some of the fathers celebrated on the weekend after a hard week of work, having a taste of joy juice drinking or whatever made them feel good. The respect was still there. We all attended school (Ridgewood Elementary). We didn't want to be called dumb, so all the children attended school and helped each other learn.

There wasn't much to do in those days, so the children participated in the church activities. One of the activities we all had to participate in was Easter Sunday. Lizzie Mack and I gathered up all the children near and far so they could come to the church and get an Easter speech, practice it, and recite it on Easter Sunday. If the parents said they couldn't bring them to church, Lizzie and I would walk around the neighborhood and get them (we walked all over the community). The parents who attended church looked forward to seeing their children on stage. Some of them would cry, laugh, stand still, say one line, but they eventually said something once they got up front to the pulpit. The children did something because they wore their Sunday best (dressed to the hills). This may have been the first time for some of them. Some of them gained strength, but we knew every year who was going to get up there, cry, or forget their lines.

The good part of all this was that the children gained strength, and the stage fright diminished. Today, some of those children who cried every year are now preachers and teachers, leaders of youth groups, law enforcement, and many other professions.

The other activities we participated in were the Girl Scouts and Boy Scouts. We played baseball in our homemade parks on our street before houses were built in some areas. Lawton Street had its own park. We played on empty lots and kept them clean. It is amazing how we, as children, did things on our own, but there was nothing else to do.

"Life ain't no crystal staircase, but I keep on climbin'." -Langston Hughes.

v

"Although poor and happy, Still I Rise."
-Maya Angelou.

"I have always loved the eloquence of simple people. What they say, coming from the heart, often goes straight to the heart." -Archibald Rutledge.

There isn't a day that goes by that I say I have got to finish writing this book. Someone is always saying somebody needs to write about Ridgewood. My reply has been, I'm writing it, and I am going to finish it one day. As I think back on my parents and siblings and the people in the community, I feel compelled to write and not stop until the book is complete.

All the quotes above depict how I grew up and my determination to strive to be more than what we lived among. I've always wanted to be somebody great. I wanted to make contributions to the community and the world. I was never selfish; I always wanted my friends to be a part of what I was going to become. This meant I wanted to do good, but I also wanted them to do good.

Chapter 1

The Community

I was born in a small community known as Ridgewood. Before that, it was called Ridgewood Heights. A family of twelve children in a neighborhood that was called the ghetto. It was not a ghetto to me at all. Everyone in the community lived the same. Some had more than others, but we were all poor. I like to say remove the "or" we were "po," but most importantly, we were all happy.

As a little girl, growing up in a community where nearly everybody had an outside toilet (a few houses had bathrooms), one pump to get water (with the exception of a few who had a well), and a four room house. If you were lucky, you may have had a house with five or six rooms, depending on when it was built.

The others were shotgun houses. The shotgun houses consisted of three rooms, and you could look straight through, from the front door to the back door. There was one grocery store, Mrs. Holloway's, and one elementary school, Ridgewood Elementary School, for blacks only.

The Elementary School went from the first to the

sixth grade, and one high school, Eau Claire High, went from the 7th to the 11th and later the 12th grade. The kicker was that the high school was in the middle of a mixed community, mostly blacks, but the school was for whites only. The black children had to leave the community by way of the city bus to go to Booker Washington High School, several miles away. In later years, W. A. Perry was built, a middle school that consisted of seventh and eighth grades.

The black children who were old enough to go to high school had to be bused to C. A. Johnson or Booker T. Washington High Schools. The children who attended C. A. Johnson High caught a school bus, and the children who attended Booker T. Washington High had to catch a city bus. During those days, you attended one of the schools according to which side of the railroad tracks you lived on. But prior to that, Booker Washington was the only black school you could attend until the middle school was built. There was one church on Ridgeway Street, Ridgewood Baptist Church. The church was first named Ridgewood Colored Church. Then, there was a little Holiness church on Woodbrier Street, which was in the upper part of Ridgewood.

It is amazing how much love was generated in the community, even more so on Lawton Street. At one time, Lawton Street was called Green Street because the Greens were the first family to move into the neighborhood. The street was a dirt road until the late 1950s, but so were all the streets in the community. There was so much love in that community that when outsiders came to the neighborhood, they thought that everyone was related. As you look at the family names, you will find that many of the families were related.

The families migrated from Jenkinsville, Winnsboro, Richtex, Cedar Creek, Hopkins, Swansea, and Eastover. When you spoke of someone in Ridgewood, it was a good idea to ask who the parents were (*who your mama* or *who your people are*) because if not, you might be talking about someone's mama, daddy, sister, brother, or cousin.

Sidenote: C.A. Johnson High School

Known locally as "C.A.J.," the high school located on Barhamville Road opened in 1949 and was dedicated the following year to Cornell Alvin Johnson, supervisor at that time of Columbia's African American schools. Johnson was a giant in the segregated educational system of Columbia, beginning his career as a teacher at Howard School in 1914, the city's first—founded in 1869—and, for many years, the only African American school. When Johnson taught English at Howard, the school had a student body of about 900 students and twenty-five teachers, all housed in the two-story frame building. C.A.J. High School opened initially with a capacity for both junior high and high school students and was intended to relieve crowding at nearby Booker T. Washington High School.

Alumni of C.A.J. remember the school for fostering a strong work ethic and challenging academics and providing a solid base of support from committed teachers and staff. Perhaps one of C.A.J.'s most famous graduates, Charles Bolden Jr., credits his high school alma mater with serving as a "model" for his successful career as a Major General in the U.S. Marines, a NASA astronaut, and an administrator.

~Courtesy of historiccolumbia.org

Chapter 2

Families of the Community

All the families on Lawton Street were large. As I became older, I found that the American dream family, so the whites say, was your parents and two children (a boy and a girl). Well, that never happened on Lawton Street. My family consisted of my parents, eight girls and four boys with me being the tenth child. We lived in a three-room house in Reuben's Alley, and prior to that, we lived in Cedar Creek on Montgomery Road and later on Bookman Loop near my grandma, aunts, and uncles. In those places, they lived in a three-room house. There were nine people. After moving to Columbia, the living conditions were no better. There were ten children in that house and later twelve. The house had wooden windows (windows that closed and opened like a door) with hinges on them. When my parents or older siblings opened the windows, there were no window panes or screens, and anything could fly in (just open space).

There were cracks in the walls, so you could look outside anywhere in the house. There were cracks in the floorboards, so wide you could see the chickens running back and forth under the house. If the chickens were running loose and didn't use the chicken coop, you could even see where the eggs were laid.

In the afternoon, my older siblings had to run and catch the chickens and put them in the chicken pen to keep the dogs or foxes from eating them.

The first time I went to the country to visit my grandma, it was so much fun because my younger brother and I had an opportunity to run after the chickens to see if we could catch them. We had nothing else to do; we were so tired that all we could do was eat dinner and go to bed. We didn't have a bathroom, so there was no bath during the week. We would eat, go to bed, and start over the next day doing the same thing.

Chapter 3

The Layout of the House

My, what a layout! Now, I know everyone's wondering how in the world that many children slept in a three-room house. Well, it was like this: My dad and ma slept in the first room of the house, which was also the entrance into the house. There was a double iron bed, a chest-of-drawers, and a long chair (that's what we called it then; today, it is called a sofa), and this was also the living room.

The children slept in the middle room. There were two double beds, one for the boys and one for the girls. There was a system. In the boy's bed, the older ones slept at the head and the two youngest at the foot of the bed. Now, for the girls it was really crowded, three at the head and four at the foot. My baby brother slept in the bed with my parents. There was a fireplace in the front room and a fireplace in the middle room. The last room was the kitchen, which consisted of a stove, a long wooden table made by my dad, two long wooden benches, and a refrigerator, which was called the icebox and that is exactly what it was.

There was a space for a block of ice to keep the

inside cool and you didn't stand there with the door open because the ice would melt. The Westside Ice Company "ice man" in the refrigerated ice truck came through the neighborhood selling blocks of ice every day. The price was fifty cents for a large block and twenty-five cents for a small one. To this day, the Westside Ice House still remains on Laurel Street.

When the family moved from Richtex to Ridgewood in 1943, we moved to a street called Reuben Alley. The house was in the same condition, but the difference was that the older siblings had gotten smarter on how to keep warm. They had newspaper and cardboard boxes to put on the wall to cover the cracks in the wall. The floors in Reuben Alley were better; they did not have real large cracks. When I tell you we were poor, we took the 'or' off poor, we were *po*, but so was everyone else. We didn't know the difference. We didn't have electric lights. We had a lamp that burned kerosene oil, so you know, when night came, it was dark, and all you saw were small flicks of light all through the community.

You prayed you didn't have to go anywhere when it got dark. The only thing you could do was go home and stay there. The other thing you prayed for was no rain because when it rained, you had plastic that you would put over your cover to keep from getting wet. Pots were sitting all through the house where the leaks were. The house had a tin roof, so if you got a leak and didn't have money to buy tar to cover the hole, in came the rain. I used to hear people talk about going to the beach and lying on the beach to look up at the stars. Well, guess what? I didn't have to go to the beach because when I went to bed every night, I could look up through the ceiling, see the moon, and count the stars. As I said earlier, when my family left Richtex, there were nine children. I was born in Ridgewood, and so were my younger brother and a sister who lived only two weeks after her birth.

Mrs. Murphy delivered most of the children in Ridgewood. The midwife's responsibility was to write down when the children were born, their names, and who the parents were, and she carried the information to the clinic to be recorded. All of us were delivered by a midwife. Ten of the children were delivered by my grandmother, Mrs. Ella Trapp, and the other two by Mrs. Maggie Murphy.

Records were kept in the family Bible, and when you needed a birth certificate, you could go to the Richland County Health Department (*The Clinic*) to get it. When you were ready to go to school, if the information was not recorded at the clinic, the parent would take the bible and let the clerk see it, and that was how you got the birth certificate. Sometimes, when you went to get the information, it was not right. Your name might be spelled wrong, your date of birth might not be right, well, that was what you were stuck with.

During those days, if there were complications when the baby was born, someone with a car – there was one or two in the neighborhood – would go to the doctor's office and let the doctor know, and the doctor would make a home visit. I remember we had Dr. Allen, a white doctor, in Eau Claire Town Hall, the only doctor I knew. He was there for most of my life.

Later, we learned about two black doctors, Dr. C. E. Spann and Dr. Steve Stephenson, who practiced on Oak Street. We had two Columbia hospitals. The one facing Hampton Street was for whites only, and the one on Harden Street was for blacks (back then, it read *For Coloreds)*. The hospital names were Waverly, for colored people, and Columbia Hospital on Harden Street. If you had Dr. Spann or Dr. Stephenson as your doctor, you had to go to Waverly because segregation was alive and well. Not to say that it is not today. It has not gone anywhere, just dressed in a suit.

Chapter 4

The Outside Toilets

We lived in a community, as I said earlier, where most of the families had outside toilets. Knowing this might sound gross, but if you had to use the toilet, the bathroom as we know it now, we had to go outside, and God forbid if it was at night. As a small child, you would be scared to death, so you would get one of your sisters to go with you. We didn't have flashlights, so whoever went with us would get a piece of paper, most of the time, a brown paper bag that we had saved from the grocery store. Sometimes, it was the newspaper that your mama had gotten from her job or someone in the neighborhood who took the State newspaper, which was not many. Then, you would light the paper so you could see where you were going. Also, you used the lit paper to make sure there were no snakes or spiders on the seat. You prayed you didn't have to go to the toilet more than once at night.

If you are wondering about the outside toilet: well, it was a small little house with a door and a hole in the ground with a wooden box built around the hole and a wooden cover over the hole with a seat on it. When you went into the toilet as a younger child, you would always say, "Don't let me fall in the hole." So, whoever went with you at night would sit you on the seat to make sure you didn't fall in. As years passed, my ma got a big bucket for us to urinate in, but if you had to do a number two (a bowel movement), well, you still had to go outside to the toilet.

My family did not get a bathroom until I got my first job, which was in 1963. I had a bathroom installed in our house. Before the bathtub, we had to bathe in a tin tub two or three times a week. We would heat the water on the side of the wooden stove, which was the cooking stove with a tank on the side of it. We would make a fire in the stove, and while Mama was cooking, we would go get water from the pump, fill up the tank, and use the hot water from the stove to place in the tub to bathe in. At least five or six of us would take a bath using the same tub and water. Sometimes, the older children would bathe first, and the little children had to be last. If you didn't bathe during the week when Saturday came, you really had to take a bath on Saturday night for Sunday church.

An Outdoor Toilet

Chapter 5

How We Survived

I know many are wondering how our parents made it. There were many entrepreneurs in the community. Some were legal, and some were illegal. We had singers on Lawton Street, runners, hairdressers, beauticians, electricians, you name it, we had it. Leila Mae and Thelma did the young children's hair for Easter. When they finished, sometimes your head would be on fire. They would say, "Hold still" or "You gonna git burn," that was an ear or scalp. The straightening comb was so big.

We also had beauty shops in the neighborhood, but we couldn't afford to go, so the older girls did our hair.

My dad worked for the railroad and later for Richtex Brick Company. This is where most of the men in the community worked. They could walk to work because it was not that far. My mama washed clothes for white families that lived in the neighborhood. My dad made eleven dollars a month working on the railroad and about seven dollars a week at the brickyard. My mama made three dollars a week washing and ironing clothes for whites in the community.

Let me tell you about washing the white clothes. My older sisters and brothers had to get the water from the pump that was in our backyard and fill the wash tub with water, three of them. There was one for washing, one for rinsing, and one for bluing. The bluing was a blue stick that dissolved in the water, which made the clothes look whiter. If there was a large number of sheets to wash, then there was the wash pot. Mama used to put the sheets in the wash pot, boil them, and then rinse them.

What is a wash pot? A round iron pot. It is black or brown in color, with three or four small legs on it. When she got ready to use it, my brothers placed bricks under each leg to make it higher off the ground. Then, they would place wood under the bottom of it, place water in the pot, and make a fire. Once the water was hot, she would put the clothes in it to boil…about thirty minutes. Once the clothes were boiling, My Ma had a long stick to turn the clothes, as if you were stirring a pot of food. Once they had boiled for about thirty minutes, she would take them out with the stick and then place them in the rinse water. She also used the Pot to make Lye soap, for bathing and washing clothes. It was used to cook crackling skins when they killed a hog. We're still alive after all the things that pot was used for.

Can you imagine how much water they had to pump

to fill the three tin tubs and the wash pot? I was glad I was the younger girl because I was too small to do that. That was one way our family survived. During those days, fifteen dollars went a long way.

A Wash Pot

The other way our family made it was that my dad always had a garden, and we grew a lot of our food. We had hogs, chickens, goats, and a cow for milk and to make butter. One thing about that neighborhood, the men knew my dad worked out of town a lot and some of them would come and work the garden. When the food was ready to be harvested, many of them came back to get food.

Many gardens were planted in Ridgewood, some on other people's properties. One gentleman, Mr. Gantt, had about four or five gardens planted all over the community. When the time came for harvest, he would gather his children, and they would deliver food everywhere. Everybody had food. If someone knew a family was without food, they would take them food or fix a meal, and the children would deliver it to them. There was no charge.

There were a lot of hog pens in Ridgewood. This is funny telling it like it was. One man on our street would feed his hogs early Sunday morning, and the next time you would see him, he'd be dressed to the nines in a suit and tie and ready for church.

Different families would kill hogs when it got cold, and some of the men in the neighborhood would help with the hog killing and cleaning. The women, five or six of them, would come to help clean the chitterlings, make sausage, and cook the crackling. The crackling was cooked in the wash pot. Like most of the families in the neighborhood, once the hog was finished, my dad would share the food with others.

Then, there were the chickens that would be cooked for Sunday. The chicken was put in a separate cleaned coop before it was killed. Dad or Mom would wring the chicken's neck off, place it in boiling water in the wash pot to take the feathers off, gut it, and thoroughly clean it inside and out. Every week, we had chicken for Sunday dinner.

We ate vegetables from the garden. My Dad would go hunting with some of the men in the neighborhood.

They would kill rabbits, squirrels, possums, and raccoons, but most of us wouldn't eat those. My brothers and other young men in the community would also hunt, and to this day, they still go hunting for rabbits. That day of sharing is gone, but we can never forget the love that was shared in Ridgewood.

My Mother "Mrs. Leila's Original Iron

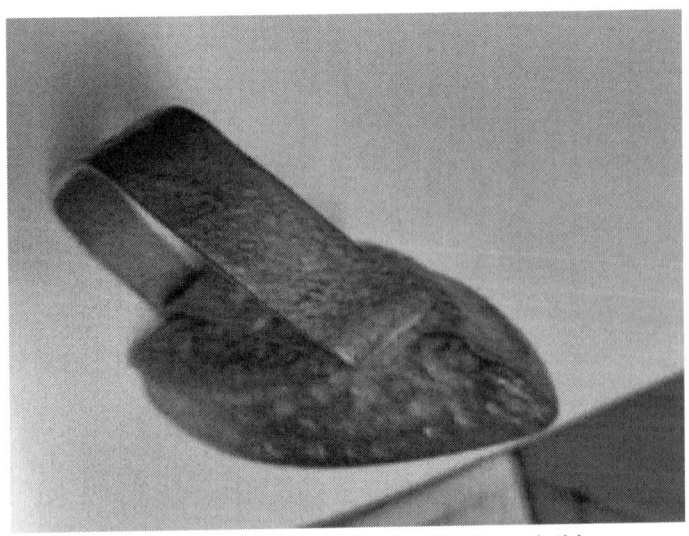

The original iron my mom used to iron clothing.

Chapter 6

The Big Move, "Those that can do, those that can't, watch."

"Quote from "Archie Stewart "

"Archie always says, if you ain't got it but want it and can't afford it, you have to watch the people that got it already and wish." After living in Reuben Alley for four or five years, we moved to Lawton Street, where we had four rooms but still an outside toilet. We didn't have holes in the wall in that house, but there was no insulation. So, you could imagine how cold it still was, but the conditions were better. There were more houses on the street, more children living closer to you, and we had electric lights.

The toilet was still on the outside but was new and better built. You could not tell us that we were not living in high cotton. When we moved to Lawton Street, the house was built high off the ground, and we played under the house. Most of the children on the street also came to play there. As children, we were entrepreneurs. Everything we played with, we made. All of the wise tales that went along with our making came from our older sisters, brothers, and other older children in the neighborhood; we believed them.

Some of the toys we made took all day. I guess our older siblings, who were the babysitters, didn't mind because they knew where we were and didn't have to look out for us as much. We made our dolls out of Coke bottles. We pulled up grass and washed it off until the roots were clean and stringy, then stuck it in the bottle with a stick.

Some made doll hair from the silk on the inside of the corn. You know how well that held up and how long it lasted. Some were made from rope if you could find it. We made high-heeled shoes from tin cans that our parents threw in the trash. We would put them on the back of our shoes and walk in them - playing like we were adults. We made our wagons by using the wheels from old wagons, tricycles, bikes, or scooters and placing a piece of wood in the middle. Sometimes, we made high-back wagons because the only thing we could find was two large bike wheels.

We made rick racks from pieces of wood that we got when the woodman delivered the wood. We would find a thin piece and chip the sides of the wood to fit our hands with a hatchet. A hatchet is a smaller version of an axe. Then, we would find an old golf ball with cuts in it and make a fire to take the top off of the golf ball. Once the cover got hot, it would pop off, and we would take it out of the fire so we wouldn't burn the rubber around the golf ball. Once the ball cooled down, we would take the rubber and unravel it long enough to place it on the wood with a nail. Then, we would punch a hole in the ball with a nail and use a stick to put the rubber in the hole. Then, tie the rubber around the ball so the rubber can extend when it hits the piece of wood for your Rick Racks.

This is funny. Our siblings would tell us when we were making our rick racks not to let the white stuff get in our eyes or faces because it was poison. So, you know that scared us. "They never said don't play with fire because you might get burned."

We played jackstones with rocks and a rubber ball from the inside of the golf ball. If we were energetic that day, we would get two.

How did we get the golf balls? Well, our brothers worked at the Ridgewood Golf Club, which was in our neighborhood. They would bring old balls home for us to play with. I guess you could call our house the community shop because we made things under the house, rain or shine. We were young inventors and didn't know it. Most of the time, no one got hurt, and if they did, we would say blow it or kiss it because if we cried, we would have to stop making our toys.

As I think more about the toys we made and played

with, I realize that we never saw anyone play those games. We were too young to go to town, and we didn't have a television, so we made things up.

When we were old enough to go to the Five and Ten stores and see the games, that was amazing. We had a Five and Dime in the neighborhood, but we rarely saw the toys that we made. When we did see them, we wanted to buy them, but whoever we were with would say, "You play that already; we don't have the money."

Chapter 7

Families Helping Families

Because the families were large, there were more children to play with. I have mentioned family names because they meant the world to me, and I want them to know that I remembered them. All of them made an impact on my life in some way. They taught me many lessons. As a child, I learned how to bond, build relationships, how to build things, how to choose my friends, how to trust and where to go to get help when needed. We learned from each other, and some of our associates were not honest; they didn't want to learn. We learned early on that as we grew, some of them would not be good adults, slow to learn, in trouble with the law, and so on.

These were families that I recall living on Lawton Street. There were the Elkins children, four of them .Then we had the Watkins family; there were eight of them, but there were only four that we could play with because the others were older. There were the Lawhorns, four of them, and we could play with three of them. Then there were the Macks, seven of them, and we could play with two of the children.

Then there were the Spanns, who had six children and one granddaughter, who was being raised by her grandmother, and we could play with two of them.

O. Trapp had one child. The Pringles and Lyles lived next door. They had eleven children. The Pringles moved to Lawton Street after the Lawhorns built another house with more rooms across the street from their first house.

There was the Bethel Family, which included four children to play with. The Johnsons had five children that we could play with and or babysit. The Callahan's had five children and we could play with three of them. There was the Pearsons, two brothers who lived side by side. One had five children, and the other had two. Of the Pearsons, we had only one child to play with. The Page Family had four but there was only one that we could play with.

Mrs. Martha Pearson lived on the corner, she lived alone for a long time. She had a tall wooden fence around her house. The amazing thing about her yard was that she had lots of plum trees, and when it was plum season, you had to beg for plums. She had a son who lived on Ridgeway Street. They had eight children. The McIlwains had four. The Gates had no children. I lived with them for six years. In later years, they had one child. The Salters had one child.

The Reese family had six children, the Halter family

had nine, the Bethel family on Ridgeway Street had five, the Geter family had six, the Thompsons had six, the Taylors had six, the Williams had three, and the Taylor family in Rubin's Alley had three. The Mitchells had seven.

The families living in Sylvia Circle and Ridgeway Street.

The Prophets had four children. The Tuckers had seven children. The Nelsons had seventeen. The Lide family had five children. The Bannisters had one child. The Darby family had four. The Geters had three. The Drehers had nine children. They lived on Lawton Street before moving to Sylvia Circle. The Whites had two. The Yarboroughs had two. The Davises had five. The Thomases had five.

The Johnsons lived on the lower part of Ridgeway Street and had four children. The Strongs had one child. The Sumter's had four children. The Tolberts had two.

The Taylors lived on the lower part of Lawton Street had four and later three more when they moved to another house on Ridgeway Street. As time passed and some families moved on, the young adults married; we had more children to play with.

The Beltons moved next door to us, and it was seventeen of them, and we could play with eight of them. The Dixons had five children, one special needs child, and we would go down to their house to speak to him. Their dad did odd jobs everywhere, and we could go and get junk from their yard to make things to play with. Later, we had the Brown family, and there were six children.

The Hollis family lived on Lawton Street, and they had two children at that time, but later they moved.

Several families on the street had no children. The Johnson, Friday, and C. Trapp families. I would say they were the second mothers and fathers to all the children on the street because, after a certain hour, you could not go past their house if your parents were not at home.

In later years, we had the Allen family; there were six children. They moved. The Beltons moved into the house. To that union, four children were born. Later, two more children were added to the family, and shortly thereafter they moved.

The Taylors had seven children. The Boyles had seven children. They moved, and the Davis family moved into that house, and five children were born to that union. The Johnsons had seven children when they moved to Lawton Street. Then, if you went to Friday's Alley, you had Mrs. Rose Hill. Her grandson lived with her. She lived across the street from her son. The Hills had five children. The Lakin Family had three children.

The Brown Family had one child. The Outen family had two children. The Wise Family had two children.

Mrs. Hun raised her two grandchildren. Her son, who lived on the corner of Friday's Alley and Monticello, had fourteen children. We could play with six of them. The Folks had three children. The James had five children, but we only played with one. The Ashfords had three.

As you move up Ridgeway Street…

The Lewis family had three children. The Pearsons had two children. The Tuckers had three children. The Moons had five children. The Macks had two children. The Youngs had eight children. The Green family lived close together, and there were many of them. One family had two, one had three, and one family had one. The Watkins had eight. The Davis family had seven. The Robertsons had three. The Davises had one child. The Floyds had two children. The Goodwins had two, and the Martins had three children. The Robertson family lived close together even after marriage.

The Jacksons had one son. The Gills had seven. The Moons had five. Mrs. J. Davis had one. The Etheridge had seven. The Samuels had fourteen. The Davises had two. There were a lot of Davises in the upper part of Ridgewood. Then we had the J.M. Davis. There were four of them. The Chandlers had nine.

The Calhouns had six children. The Taylors had two. The other Taylors had one. The McCartys had five.

The Cutners had three, The Colemans two. The Greens had three. The Porters had one, and the Butlers had five. The Williams had six, the Dixons had four, the Whites had three children, and the Fords had one.

The Davolls had five or six. The Veals had two. The Davises had nine. The Richardsons had two. Mrs. Rachel had two. The Jones had two. The Greens had two, and the Wise family had three. The Tuckers had five or six, the Watkins had three, the Hoefers had four, and the Reeds had four.

The Fergusons had three. The Williams had one, the Thompsons had four, and the Salvages had seven. The Hipps had three, the Boyds had two, the Goings had one, and the Harrisons had six. The Kings had two, the Boyles had three, the Wilsons had six, the Pleasants had none, the Hills had seven, the McNeills had seven, and the Nelsons had none.

These were the three white families in the community. The Clarks, the store owner, didn't have any. The Butlers, store owners, had one, and Mr. Brown, the store owner, had one.

The Knightners, lived on Knightner Street. There were seventeen of them. Mama Lillie (Mama Lia) was like the little mayor and could be seen all over the community; what she said and did was the law. So much respect was shown to her.

The Gladdens had fourteen, the Turnipseeds had

three, the Trapps had eight, the Monroes had one, the Evans had five, the Thompsons had three, the first Caldwell family had two children, and the other Caldwells had one. The Zimmermans had five, the Golds had six, the Whetstones had three, the Byrds had one, the Gantts had four, the Gantts had seven, and the Crums had four.

Mrs. Williams had none, the Bickleys had two, the Cornelius family had three, Mrs. White had none, the Bethels six, the Wilsons one, the Wannamakers had seven or eight, and the Mitchells had five.

It is not my intent to leave anyone out. If I have, charge it to my head and not my heart. I have tried to go as far back as I could to remember the families and let them see how the community has diminished over the years. The one thing I can say about the neighborhood is that there were many babies to babysit, and there was no pay involved. You learned at an early age to care for others. Our parents used to say all the time, "Don't look to get paid for everything you do because you will be blessed for what you do for others."

Some families lived in a shotgun house similar to this one. According to some folks, the shotgun house got its name from its long, narrow design, theorizing that a bullet shot through the front door could exit the back door. Other folks said you could stand at the front door and look straight through to the back door.

Chapter 8

Nicknames

Everybody on Lawton Street and most of Ridgewood had a nickname. Some of them will crack you up, and today, they will tell you not to tell anybody what I was called when I was growing up. A thing that you learned early to live with was the name the community gave you.

Sometimes, you didn't learn the person's birth name or, as we say, their government name, until they died. If their nickname wasn't given, you didn't know who they were talking about. Nicknames meant a lot in the black community. Every so often, you were given a name because of your behavior. This means if you did nice things, you got a name; if you thought you were bad or a bully, you got a name to describe you, as well. If you were a bully, most of the time, the kids would stay away from that person because they knew they would have to fight or get in trouble. And there were times you were given nicknames because of your living conditions.

When I talk about living conditions, we were all poor, but some were poorer than others. As I mentioned earlier, we all could take "or" off of "poor" because we were "po". Your looks could get you a name. Children can sometimes be mean, but you couldn't be that way around the adults, so they came up with a name and laughed. However, the adults didn't know what was going on, so the name stuck. There were times when children would be given a name; they would cry. That was one of the ways they would change their behavior so they could get a better name. That didn't happen often. Amazingly enough, the names did affect the person. Some of the people in the community, when they became older, would tell you, don't call me that anymore. I have changed, and that name doesn't go well with me.

These are some of the names, I will not give the real names of the people that they belong to because I know they would choke me to death:

Son, Nicki Bow, Brother, Boy, Shorty, Cooter, Dudley, De-Duly, Honeypie, Son, Jake, Little Charles, Tuff Man, Bad Foot, Fat Man, Jimbo, Big Rabbit, Tata, Ro, Ms. Sweet, Moon-Shine, Pete, Lips, Bookie, Dolt, Skeetieboo, Jr Boy, Toot Boy, Cat, Sister, Sudha, Junior, Brown, Row, Lilliebell, Ruth Boy, Ninnie Reese, Slim, and Son Boy.

Miss Nunk, Monkey Pee, Little Son, Mookie, Monkie Hill, Thea, Bow Biscuit, Major Brown, Black Gal, Miss Hun, Miss Mac, Mr. Rev, Billy Bump, Red,

Bubba Outon, Hoober Jr., Sonny Boy, Dot, Dot-Belly, Mr. Willie the Fireman, Crip, Pretty Popper, Mooney, Bobby, JC, AJ, Sam-Bo, Joe Black, Sonny Boy, Mo Pig, Mo-Hickie, and Buck.

Taunt, Squeaky, Gina, Tub, Dooley, Honey Baby, Ma-Joe, Pooches Gal, Mookie, Hun Wise, Ms. Honey, Mr. Biggie, Ms. Sissy, Jo, Mr. Pick, Ms. B, Molly, Nickie, Lil Louis, Boogie, Chicken Hatten, Bear Wise, Skeet-A-Boy, and Flat-Foot.

Bookie, WJ, Tit-eye, May-libber, Mr. Son, Shine, Peanut, Pop Trapp, Tiny-bee, Mr. Precious, Pat, Jean, Prissy, Jo, Coo Coo, Goat, Lue, Chilly Willie, Favbalue, and many of the families had a "Sister" in the house.

There were a lot of Bobbies. We would call many of the adults in the community by their full name. If you didn't, the next thing you knew, you were getting punished for being disrespectful. The families in Ridgewood continued to give their children nicknames as years passed. I guess it was a way of showing love to the children.

Someone would give them a name and it stuck. I was upset because I didn't have a nickname. There were maybe two or three others who didn't have nicknames. I guess we were very special.

Chapter 9

The Porch School

We had families in the neighborhood that lived better than some of us but were still poor. They shared everything: food, clothing, shoes, money, you name it. Then, we had our neighborhood school teachers. Our neighborhood school teacher at the age of ten or twelve, give or take a year, was Dr. Catherine Spann Davoll. Every day around three or four o'clock and sometimes later if it was hot or the weather was bad, we had to go to the Spann's house to play school. This was one of the best things that could have happened.

Catherine taught us how to count, learn our ABCs, read, and write. Most of the children that went there were between the ages of three to six. When you went there, all the children would start at the top of the steps. There was no order of teaching. She would just ask simple things. She would begin by asking, "What did you learn yesterday," and if you could tell her, she would say, "You pass," and would let that person or persons move down to the next step. Then she would start her class and ask a question," "What comes after A?" If you answered correctly, you passed. Then, she would say, "I have a rock in my hand, and if you can guess which hand it is in, I will pass you to the next step."

After that, she would bring out the blackboard, which is now called the chalkboard. Their dad had made this small board to teach them how to write, and she would bring it out for school. She was always very smart. She would start by making a line on the board and would say, *how many lines do you see?* If we didn't know how to count, no one would say anything; she would say one, then she would draw another line and say two, and so on.

Then she would look at our hand and say, *let's count your fingers on your hand and then your toes.* This is how we learned to count. She would tell us the parts of our body, and when we were old enough to go to school, we knew what a first grader needed to know if we attended her class. We didn't have kindergartens or nurseries during those days. She shared with us what she learned as a young child, and it prepared us for the future.

The flip side to this is that when we started going to school, it didn't stop there. We still had to go to the Spanns' house every day after school to play school with Catherine. Sometimes, her mother would make Kool-Aid drinks or sugar biscuits for us. She told us at an early age, "You need to go to school to learn and be smart and go to college."

The good part about all of this is that she not only taught us at an early age, but it also inspired her to become an educator as an adult. She was a great educator. She was also a great friend and helped many of us in the community complete school. She was a great asset to the community and church.

Chapter 10

Neighborhood Protection

We never saw a sheriff unless they were riding through the community to go to some other place. Our parents were our protection. If a child did something bad, the parent would tell the child's parent and they would discipline the child, and that was the end of that situation. If a child stole something from a store, they had to go to that store and admit they had stolen something. They had to clean the yards of that business or something, and then they would get a beat down from their parents or someone's parents, it all depends on who was watching you while your parents weren't at home.

The store owners never called the police on the children because they knew the parents would handle it. We had several nightclubs. If a fight broke out and it was bad and the men couldn't break it up, then the owner would call the sheriff. Every once in a while, if someone got too drunk and no one could stop them from acting out, a neighbor would call the sheriff. Usually, this was on the weekend.

One thing about those days was that men had to

work every day to take care of their families. There were no Social Services available to our community.

Then, there were times when we had visitors. The Ku Klux Klan (KKK) would ride through the neighborhood to scare the blacks. The men in the neighborhood handled that also. One night, they came and burned a cross. They said they would be back the next night and do it again. They came back, and some of the men were waiting for them. Most of the men in the neighborhood were hunters; they went to the location and waited. The KKK came, and several of the men had their shotgun and bird pellets and shot up the pick-up truck. We never had that problem again.

The people in the community always thought that the Clarks, who owned the Grocery store, were part of the KKK. Archie, a young man who visited the community, would say, "It ain't no fun when the rabbit got the gun." True, true, true.

We had family fights, and they were big fights if more than one family member jumped on a child. That was one of those situations where they may say *may the best man win*. Once the fight was over, that was it. The families were back together the next day.

Ridgewoodians protected each other. If you didn't live in the community and started something, all the Ridgewoodians around had your back.

The weekends were always something to look

forward to. Several men had their joy juice (whiskey) early. They would act out with one another and then go home. That was the end until the next week. Some of the ladies in the community were abused, and they knew that they could come to our house, and my dad would not let their husbands bother them.

Chapter 11

Neighborhood Entertainment

Everyone on Lawton Street could sing. Mr. Leroy lived on the corner of the street, and he would sit on his porch after work and start singing. All the other families would be on their porches, and all the children on the street would run that way. We would line up like we were on the usher board or choir in church and start singing with Mr. Leroy, and we would march up and down the dirt road.

We had runners. Sudha was the fastest runner, and we used to say she ran fast because of her bow legs. The guys on the street would challenge her, but they couldn't outrun her. As I became older, I would run, and we had others that would run. Finally, I did outrun her - once. We would have races down the street, and there was this young man who would race with us. He was fast. We would say you need to run track in school. He did run track in school and was the fastest in the state for the years he participated.

There was a special electrician (fake) - not the kind that repairs things. The real electrician was Frankie Jr.

Every day, we would play this electric game. Frankie Jr would tell us to line up, and we did. Then he would say wet the spot at the end of the line. There would be as many as twenty-five children lined up, and he would say, "Who was bad today?" We would say who it was. He would make that person stand in the wet spot. Then he would stick his finger in the electrical outlet, the electricity would run all the way down the line to the person on the end, and it would really shock them. We would disconnect to keep that person from getting shocked too bad. It took our parents a long time to figure out what we were doing. When they did, we were punished in some way, beaten down, like somebody had stole something.

As faith would have it, God took care of us because each one of us could have been shocked to death. Nevertheless, those were the games we played.

After going to the Spanns for school, if we left early, then we would go to the Trapps, under the edge of the house, and we could play a game called hack-a-pack-a-doodle. This was a hole in the ground, and when we found one, we would get a stick and stir in the hole until a bug appeared. We played Hide and Seek, Little Sally Walker, Ring Around the Roses, Hot and Cold, Samson, May I, Marbles, and anything else that would make a game. We jumped roped Double Dutch and single jump rope.

Estelle Trapp Young

The older guys played cards, Bid Whist, Spaces, other card games, and checkers. The checkerboard was made on a wooden panel. It was painted black and white and sometimes black and red. The other thing that was different about Lawton Street was that most of the families had a piano. The Spann children and several of the Trapp children took music lessons. The Young family lived on Ridgeway Street, and everyone in their family could really play. We could go to anybody's house and get on the piano. The Trapp family also had a pump organ.

Marbles and Jacks

We played Jack Stones with rocks, and later, we found out about Jacks. Once we were able to buy Jacks with a ball, when we lost a Jack, we added rocks. Every house had a special function. The Watkins was the house of laughter, and the Macks were the first family on Lawton Street to have a television. In the afternoon all the children went there to watch "It's Howdy Dodie Time".

At the Lawhorn house, if you needed to go anywhere, Mr. Frank was the taxi cab driver. The Dixons had the carpenter if you needed something built. Mrs. Elkins was the cake baker. The Trapp's and Mack's house was the cafeteria; everybody came to their house to eat all the time, but anybody on Lawton Street would feed you. The Trapp's house was also a place of fun. Mrs. Bea, Mrs. Mac, and Mrs. Pinkey stopped the children from going to Monticello Road because it was a busy street, and they didn't want anyone to get hit by a car.

Everybody had a long porch, for what it was worth. The families didn't have fans, so everybody would gather on their porch after work and watch all the children play in the dirt road. We would skate in the dirt, but on the weekend, we could go on the Ridgewood Camp Road to skate well because it was paved. If you got hurt, you better not cry because if you did, your sibling would carry you home, and you couldn't go the next time. That was your punishment. The parents on that street would look out for us if we got hurt badly and were bleeding. They would tie a rag around your leg or arm and tell you, "You will be alright and go back and skate." We walked on cans and rode in our homemade wagon. The thing we knew we had to do was be home when the sun was going down or later when the street light came on.

I would venture to say that when we were growing up, we had some of the best singers I ever heard. Mildred was the best female singer in the community. Before we knew about Aretha Franklin, Mildred could sing that way and should have made a record. Listening to her in the yard could make you cry.

Thelma could sing. They used to set the church on fire on Sundays. My brother Louis could really sing also. We had many quartet groups and a lot of programs with quartet groups from all over the city that would come to Ridgewood Church for our program. The children in the community could sing, too. We had a Junior Ushers Board, and we used to love to march around the church wall. Working in the church was a great experience.

We had a lot of entertainment. Sometimes, the children in the community would gather and play 'church', and somebody would preach. The preachers were Romeo, Charles, Frankie Jr., and Cleveland. After our service, we would find a cat or a chicken, baptize them, and shout. We would imitate some of the adults in the church who got the Holy Ghost in the church that Sunday.

On the weekend, some of the ladies in the community would come to our house and laugh and talk about things that happened to them that week or some of their friends. The younger children would sit on the porch and listen. We could listen but not say anything.

One of the ladies spoke about the day the insurance man came to her house. She didn't have the money to pay, so she told her son (who was about six or seven at the time) to "tell the insurance man I ain't. home."

The boy went to the door and said, "My mama said she ain't home."

The man said, "Where is she?"

The boy said, "In there hiding behind the door." That was a beatdown.

Another time, this was not funny what happened, but it was the way the lady told my mama about it. She said, "Leila, I have some bad news. My brother got killed last night and died this morning."

Everybody was laughing so hard. My brother said, "How are you going to get killed last night and die in the morning? It was on. My brother had to be carried to the hospital to get a shot to stop him from laughing.

One guy came to the drive-in and said, "I want a cheeseburger with cheese on it."

Growing up, you couldn't go anywhere without an

older brother or sister. One day, this little guy wanted to go to a baseball game with his uncle. The uncle told him he was going to be gone for a while, and he couldn't go this time. The little boy was crying very hard and was hurt because his uncle had never told him no before. Well, the little boy, who was about four or five, said, "Uncle Archie, Grandma said you ain't sh... and you're not."

Beat down. We have to be careful how we speak around our children because they will repeat what we say.

I don't know of many of the mothers in the neighborhood with the exception of one or two that drank, and they were a mess and funny. When they got drunk, they would dance anywhere.

It's ironic when my son was growing up, he did some of the same things with children that we did. He would play church on the church step, he would preach, and after he finished, he would take all the children down to Ms. Mac's store and buy them candy. Every Friday, when I got off work, I had to go pay Ms. Mac for Quint and Priscilla's bill. Priscilla and Gloria were always there to back Quint up. Ms. Mac would say, "That boy is gonna be a preacher." Not.

The other thing that I noticed was that the ladies in the community never wore pants to church. I don't think many of them owned a pair of pants. There was a dress code, and girls couldn't wear pants to church on Sundays, either. If you did, somebody would tell you that girls wear dresses to church. In the olden days, women had great respect for the church. But if you tell a girl or boy what they need to wear these days, you might get shot—my how things have changed.

I'm not sure if it was in other neighborhoods or not, but telephones may have come to our area in the late fifties or early sixties. Everybody was on a 'party line'. If the telephone rang, if you wanted to, you could click the phone and hear somebody's conversation. Just don't get caught doing it. If you did - a child beat down. One time, Ms. B told us about a prank call she received when we were on her porch. She said, "Estelle, you know somebody called me today and said, do you have a refrigerator? I said yes, and they said, is it running? I said yes, and they told me to go catch it. I told them I couldn't run and hung up the phone."

That was the kind of laughter we had. What a hilarious telephone system we had in those days.

Chapter 12

The Neighborhood Stores and Entrepreneurs

Ridgewood may have been several miles long, from Knightner Street to Summit Avenue and from Lawton Street to Monticello Road over to Ridgewood Camp Road over to Dixon Drive. We had several stores in the neighborhood, namely Holloways, Clark Store, Brown's Store, Butlers' Ice Cream Parlor, and Gates 5 & 10 Store.

Later in the years, we had Hollis Grocery, which was subsequently sold to Charles Henry Hills, Lucus Grocery next door, Dunn Grocery, Jake's Barbeque, Mrs. McIlwain, Ms. White's Candy Store, Mack Toddle Liquor Store, and Moss Liquor Store. I was told at one time that Mr. Charlie Williams had a Barber Shop and a Restaurant on Lawton Street. I cannot expound on this because I cannot find anyone to solidify where it was.

There were retail stores, such as Rueben's Night Club and Motel, The Renaissance Hotel, Mrs. Jimmy's Beauty Shop, Jessie Mae, Davis Beauty Shop, Martins Barber Shop, Frank Pearson Barber Shop, Gladys

Beauty Shop, Clark Liquor Store, and later Mack's Nursery, Hicks Nursery, and Brown's Barber Shop. In the later years, we had a Piggly Wiggly on Monticello Road. Rev. Walter Hollis Construction Company. Trapp's Electric Shop and Nelsons Electric, Mack Richardson's One Stop Shop, McRank's Cabinet Shop, and Belin and Nye Meat Market.

Chapter 13

The Church

Ridgewood Baptist Church: The pillow of the community Ridgewood Baptist Church was founded in 1925; the first church was started in the front yard of the Knightner Family. The Church Yard was located on Knightner Street. At that time, it was called "The Brush Habor".

The church was later moved to Ridgeway Street, and the first pastor was Rev. Zak Dennis. It was then called Ridgewood Colored Church and later Ridgewood Baptist Church.

Rev. Dennis and the men of the community built the original church. Rev Dennis was a plasterer and taught the men how to plaster, and the church was erected. It had wooden floors, a homemade podium, and homemade wooden benches. The benches had three strips of wood on the seat and three on the back, with support on both sides. We had outside toilets, one for the men and one for the women, and a built-in pool for baptism.

There was a large pot-belly stove in the corner of the

church for heating. The men would go early in the morning and build a fire for service. In the summertime, that building was so hot that there were no electrical fans; later, one big fan was purchased to place on the floor in the front of the church to cool it off. The ladies would bring a newspaper or a cardboard box cut to fan with if they didn't have a fan from a funeral home.

A large bell with a long rope was inside the church's steeple. It was rung for Sunday school and the Morning service, held twice a month. The bell was also used for funerals to let the community know the family was coming to the church. That bell could be heard a long way.

The church also had a piano. The first musician was Mrs. Franklin Harris. We had a musical choir, a Jubilee choir, and an usher board. The ushers used to sing and march around the walls every Sunday. The singing was so good, with the foot stomping and hand clapping. You could really feel the presence of the Lord. Many of the children in the community attended Sunday school. The larger children had to go and get the smaller children to take them to church and back home afterward. You talking about a village, we had one.

We had the most dedicated teachers in the world, to name a few: Mrs. Ruth Reed, Mrs. Daisy Bell Williams, Mr. B. J. Mack, Mrs. Ruby Pearson, Mrs. Rudine Pearson, Mrs. Elizabeth Holloway, Mr. Charles Trapp,

Mrs. Jesse Coleman, Mr. Louis Gates, Mr. Lovie Pearson, Mrs. Janie Hollis, Mrs. Leila Trapp, Mrs. Rosa Lee Spann, Mrs. Henrietta Green, Mrs. Rosa Hollis, Deacon Johnny Upshort, Mrs. Millie Marsh, Rev. Tally Marsh, Mrs. Frankie Harris, Malvina Pearson, Mrs. Alma Pearson. In later years, Mrs. Edna Trapp, Mrs. Dorothy Davis, Mrs. Catherine Spann Davoll, Mrs. Willie Mae Belton, Caroy Ferguson, James Hollis, Estelle Trapp Young, and James Lyles.

After Rev. Dennis's death, Rev. Jeremiah W. Witherspoon was named pastor. The church name was later changed to Ridgewood Missionary Baptist Church under the leadership of the late Rev. Levi C. Chavous, the third pastor. Many new programs were implemented and are still in place today.

Many of the people in the community attended Ridgewood Baptist, but others went back to their home church wherever they moved from. Most of the children in the community attended Sunday school, Baptist Training Unit (BTU), Vacation Bible School, and Easter programs. During the summer, we would have Tent Revival. That was a great time. Singing was heard all over the community. I can't leave out the Revival, which was held on the fourth Sunday in August and still exists to this day. Everyone looked forward to the Big Meeting, as it was called. Food was served after preaching, outside from the trunks of cars for those who had them, and picnic baskets. That was a great time. The thing that I remember most is no one ever got sick from food being out in the heat all that time. You could go from basket to basket and eat pies and cakes, chicken, potato salad, macaroni and cheese, collards, cornbread, you name it, and it was there.

Since the establishment of our church, we have had four pastors. We have also added to the church a Family Life Center and Day Care under the leadership of Rev. L. C. Chavous. Rev. Fred Coit is the present pastor of the church and continues to implement new programs.

Then we had Tent Revival maybe once or twice a year. Ms. Ag was a Tent Sister, and she would get her group to come to Ridgewood. A large tent was placed in the field, pretty much where the open space is today near the Family Life Center, and we would sing, and the preacher would preach for hours. The ladies would play the tambourine. Sometimes, to me, it was a lot of noise, but everybody went to Tent Revival.

Chapter 14

The School

Ridgewood Elementary was the only school we could attend in that area. We walked to school. When it was time for school, we would go behind the church, through the woods, on a path that our older siblings had made. Down the hill, get to the bottom, and there was a branch of water that had a big rock in the middle for you to step on to keep from stepping in the water. When it rained, the water was high, and if you didn't jump far enough, you would land in the water. We went to school for many days with wet shoes and sometimes our clothes if we fell in the water. Sometimes, you would have to go home and change clothes. Hoping you won't be late for class.

Now, the boys didn't mind because there was a long vine down there, and they would catch the vine and swing across. The smaller children were afraid to swing, so they got wet if the water was high. Sometimes, we would go up Ridgeway Street, which was the long way around. Most of the time, we went that way when we were dressed to take pictures or something special. The only other time we went the long way was when we saw a snake.

You learn something new every day if you search for it. It is amazing that we never knew how the elementary school started because no one ever talked about it. As I became older and more curious, I decided to research it. I found that the discovery from the Encyclopedia of Schools enlightened me greatly about its history.

Ridgewood School began in 1922 in a little Episcopal Church. A four-room school was built at 5300 Woodbrier Street in 1928. The first head teacher was Sallie E. Howard in 1928. She taught for 28 years. The school had two classrooms, a lunchroom, and a kitchen were added in 1948. The school had six teachers and 215 students in 1949. Mr. Norman Pendergrass was the principal. The teachers were Lillian C. Weston, Alma Williams, Marguerite Davis, Margaret Hampton, and Lizzie L. Sinclaire. Several of the teachers named were still at the school when I started in 1949.

When I think about how close-knit the community was and the "Village" we lost, many of the teachers lived in the neighborhood. We could visit them; they attended our church and were always there for us. In 1949, as mentioned in the research article, some of the students were Barbara Ashford, James Bookers, Lonnie Cheeks, Julius Dixon, Francis Dreher, Robert Folks, Jimmie Hardrick, Abraham Kennedy, Vivian Lawhorn, Robert Mack, Randolph Richardson, Willie Spann,

Arthur Taylor, Charles Trapp, Forest Tucker, and Romeo Watkins.

In 1950 and 1956 there were an addition made to the school. In 1962, John Stevenson was principal. Some of the teachers were Janie Leevy, Lily White, Mildred Dove, Rosa Williams, Mildred Page, Margaret Roache, Ora Lee Jacobs, Blondell Dixon, Rosa Williams, Margaret Middleton, and Barbara Little. The Secretary was Ms. Stewart, and the Liberian was Sadie Bailey. Mrs. Hildebrand was the cafeteria manager, and Mr. Clark was the head custodian. Jasper Salmond was principal from 1964 until he became Principal at Carver in 1968.

The enrollment was around 500 during the 1960s. Mrytle James was the principal until the school closed in 1971.

Chapter 15

The Community Stores and Other Services

The Holloway Store: The Holloway store, which is black-owned and on Ridgeway Street, has a lot of history, and you will hear me talk about it more than once. Mrs. Holloway was a Greenville native, and all the older children used to say she was a hundred years old when she moved into the neighborhood. She died at the age of 98. Mrs. Holloway sold cookies, drinks, bologna, cheese, liver pudding, bread, kerosene, candy, and plums she got out of her yard. She would allow credit to certain people. Mrs. Holloway had the best Dixie Cookies and Johnny cookies in town, and with those, we ate cheese and liver pudding.

The children went to her store most of the time for snacks. The thing about the Holloway store was you could buy one cookie for a penny or get a bag of cookies for a nickel. You could even buy a slice of cheese, bologna, and a half loaf of bread; the older children/adults would go there for Kerosene. She knew how to make money. She also taught Piano Lessons. On the weekends, she would allow certain children to come in, and she would show movies and give us popcorn and Kool-Aid.

Mrs. Holloway also had a boarding house within the building. At one time, I was informed that she rented a room to some visitors from Philadelphia. Mr. B. J. Mack stated that Sister Rosette Thorne, a well-known gospel singer, stayed there once.

Then, her family members moved in and stayed there for years. It was a place where you could go and learn to type. It was once a funeral home. She also lived within the building. At night, most of the time, the children on Lawton and Ridgeway Streets were afraid to go into the store because the older children said a ghost was in there. In later years, we had a Sunday school class there. Today, it is the Holloway/Trapp Home and is on the historical registry.

Clark's Grocery Store: The Clarks lived on the corner of Dartmouth and Monticello. Their house was on Dartmouth, and their store was on Monticello. The Clarks, we were told, came from Denny Terrace-white owners, in the middle of an all-black community. It was said more than once that Mr. Clark was a part of the KKK, and they were like the big store. They sold all kinds of meats, bread, kerosene, potatoes, to name a few things but it was a little country store. This was the main store in Ridgewood in the early 50s.

The people in the neighborhood could go to Clark's Store and credit food until they got paid. It's funny that they wrote everything down in a large ledger. Not only was this a grocery store, but when it was time for the people to vote in Ridgewood, this was the voting place. Mr. Clark also had a liquor store across the street from the grocery store. In later years, the Johnson family purchased the store, which is now a sandwich shop.

Brown's Grocery: Mr. Brown's, white-owned, was located on the corner of Summit and Monticello Road. Mr. Brown was down the street from Eau Claire school, and this is where he received a lot of his business. Mr. Brown would credit only certain people. This is funny: Ms. B said when she would get off the bus after coming from downtown, she would stop at Mr. Brown's and would tell him, "I think I'm gonna faint." He would give her ice cream to cool off. He and his family lived next door to their store. Mr. Brown also owned several houses around his store. The houses were brown in color. This was one of the main stops for the bus line. This was the beginning of the white section in Ridgewood. Once you passed Dixie Avenue, Brown was considered a part of the Eau Claire Community. The small building still stands today. It is now black-owned and is a Cajun Turkey Wing shop. Most of the families living in the area today are black. Most of the students attending Eau Claire High are black. Time did change the neighborhood.

Gates 5 & 10 Store: Gates was white-owned, located on the corner of Summit and Monticello Road. Their home was located behind the Hamburger shop, which they also owned. The Gates sold clothing, shoes, socks, curtains, spreads, sheets, hardware items, candy, cookies, brooms, mops, wash tubs, foot tubs, water buckets, dippers, toys, spoons, forks, knives, all sizes, but you had to buy them separately. This is where many families bought toys for Christmas. Didn't they know how to get over on the blacks in the neighborhood?

The owners knew many of the families didn't have vehicles, and they had to walk to most places because of a lack of transportation. They, too, had a ledger to keep their crediting customers. They also owned the Ice Cream and Hamburger shop in the early 50s and 60s. They were in the middle of a black community, but we could not go inside to order anything. We had to order from the window. The Butler Family later bought the Ice cream and Hamburger shop. However, we still couldn't enter until the late 60s when stores began to integrate.

Years passed, and Louis Trapp later purchased the store. The Trapps ran the business for a while and later rented both the store and house that was converted into a beauty shop. The 5 & 10 store was never purchased by anyone and was torn down in the early 70s.

Hollis Grocery: Hollis Grocery, black-owned, was located on Ridgeway Street at Fridays Alley in the middle of the Ridgewood Community. The Hollis family lived on St. Matthews Road. When Mr. Sammie opened his store, the community was glad because it was closer to the community of Lawton Street, Knightner Street, and Ridgeway Street. Many of the families were glad because they did not have to worry about the children going six blocks to the store. Plus, they did not have to worry about the children getting on the roadway and being hit by a vehicle. The Hollis store was major; it had everything you would need. It was the largest grocery store I had ever seen. Mr. Samuel learned that he would have to credit families' food in order to stay in business. He also did construction work and later sold his store to Charles Henry Hill.

Hill's Grocery: Hill's Grocery was also black-owned. The Hill family lived on Dartmouth Street. Charles Henry Hill took over the store, and they had a variety of foods, bread, milk, candy, vegetables, can goods in that store as well. We also had James Roland

Lyles, a brother from another mother. James Roland, that's what we called him: he lived downtown. Saturday, he worked in the store. Lyles readily became a part of our family. My mother prepared food for him every Saturday morning, and she didn't care where you had to come from or where you were; once she prepared his breakfast, we had to get it to him. Mother took Lyles as another one of her sons. Believe it or not, the adult sisters and brothers, as well as the small children, had to go to the store to give Lyles his food. I lived on Colonial Drive, and if there was no one else around, my mother would call and say, "You need to come to take Lyles his breakfast." He was very special to all of the adults in the community.

We also had Mrs. Mattie Lee, who worked in the store during the week. She lived in the community on Crest Street. She was very proper. She spoke correctly all the time, and as small children, we would say, "You from New York?" She would laugh and say no. She would always correct us. I was glad when she was there because she would make sure the children acted right in the store, and sometimes, she would talk to the young girls in the community about life. Mrs. Mattie Lee was very strict; she made sure you called her Mrs. Williams or Mrs. Mattie.

She would tell us all the time," You must learn to respect adults, and if you come in here and call me by my first name, I will not let you come back in the store until you do." If you went into the store too many times and disrespected her, she would say, "I am going to tell your mother on you." That was the magic word because if she told, you knew what followed. She knew the children and all the parents. Lesson learned. We had teachers everywhere—community people who cared for and watched over all the children in the neighborhood.

Lucas Grocery Store: Lucas's Grocery was white-owned. The Lucas family lived in Denny Terrace, and they sold groceries, but they also had hardware items and sometimes shoes (used) and other items. Mrs. Lucas used to get some of the ladies in the community to work in her house. The store was not open for a long period of time.

Dunn's Grocery: Dunn's Grocery was white-owned. The Dunn family lived on Knightner Street at Monticello Road. Dunn's had food, sold hot dogs, snow cones, beer, and wine, had a pool room, and repaired watches. It was also a main bus stop. If you were going to town and walking up Ridgeway Street, if you saw the bus, you could most likely catch it because the bus driver, most likely, had gone into the store. When Dunn first opened, you could only go in there to buy items, but you could not go into the pool room. It was for whites only. As places integrated, he later allowed blacks to go in and play pool.

Jakes Barbeque: Jakes, black-owned, was located on Ridgeway Street- next to the Lucas grocery on Ridgeway Street. This was a trailer. He would open his barbeque pit on the weekend. Many of the men in the neighborhood sat around the pit on the weekend, shooting the breeze and having fun because it gave them something to do after work. During the 4th of July weekend and Labor Day weekend, they would be up there all night cooking hogs. Mr. Jake also had a construction business, and he hired men in the neighborhood to work.

McIlwain Candy Store: McIlwain's store was black-owned and located on the corner of Ridgeway and Lawton Streets. Mr. Rev. and Ms. Mac, as they were known, had a candy store on the back of their shotgun house. Ms. Mac would let the children come into the room to get their candy, but Rev. Mac would make you stand outside, and he would show you the box of candy and sell it to you that way. They were the only store open on Sunday, so after church, all the children would go there to get candy, and the larger children and adults would go and get sodas. Later, their house was rebuilt, and they had a little room added to the side for the store. There were only four people I know Ms. Mac would credit: Ms. Beatrice, Jake Trapp, Priscilla Pelzer, and Quintus Young. Quintus had a running credit every Friday. Ms. Mac would call me if she saw me coming down the street to tell me how much their bill was. Prissy and Quin would buy candy and ice cream for the children who didn't have any money, and Ms. Mack would say, "I'm to put this on your bill," and they would say yes, ma'am. Ms. Mack would say all the time, "That boy is going to be a preacher." Not.

Rueben Night Club, Real Estate, and Motel: Reuben's was black-owned and located on Monticello Road, but it had to be entered on Knightner Street. The family lived upstairs over the nightclub. To my knowledge, this was the first nightclub in Ridgewood.

Friday, Saturday, and Sunday were the nights the older folk went there to party. Those who were the partygoers of the community. People came from all parts of the city to party at Reuben's; it was a hot spot. The piccolo was very loud and we could stand on the corner of Lawton and Ridgeway streets and hear the music. But the children were not allowed in. They sold sandwiches, candy, drinks, beer, and liquor. The Trapps owned real estate, which we used to rent from Reuben. He had houses in Reuben's Alley, Black Bottom, and many other places. As time passed, he added a motel in the backyard of his business. As children, we used to wonder what happened in those small rooms. The tales that were told were something. We used to hear the older folk talk about what happened on the weekend and who they danced with.

The Renaissance Hotel: The Renaissance was white-owned and located on Monticello Road, near Knightner Street. It had two floors. When preachers and other entertainers came to Columbia, they would stay there, so it was said, because there were no other hotels in the area for them to rent. Later, it was turned into an apartment boarding complex.

The Beauty and Barber Shops: There were beauty shops and barber shops all over Ridgewood where you could get your hair dressed or cut. Some did your hair in the home. When you went to the ladies who did hair at their house you had to wash it at home before going to get it fixed. I remember when barbers charged two dollars for a haircut, and for the women to get their hair washed, pressed, and curled was two dollars and fifty cents. Some places would charge three dollars. If it was around Easter and some of the families needed more than one child to do, sometimes the barbers and beauticians would do it for free or at a lesser cost.

Everybody cared and looked out for each other.

Mrs. Jimmy Davis was the first licensed beautician; she had one of the first beauty shops in the area that I know. She and her daughter were beauticians. Mrs. Gladys Mack rented part of the home of Mr. & Mrs. Pleasant, with a beauty shop located in the back of the house. But at that time, Mrs. Mack lived there with her husband. Frazelle had one attached to the front of her house. Jessie Mae, Thelma, Leila Mae, and Lois were the bootlegger beauticians. Estelle took cosmetology in High School and practiced on the children in the neighborhood on the weekend for free. At Easter she worked day and half the night to have the girls looking good for Easter.

Mr. Frank Pearson had the first barber shop on Lawton Street, located in the basement of his home. We later had an M&M (Mark Martin) Barbershop. Mr. Joe Davoll was a well-known barber in the area. Others who worked in the barbershop were Rev. Brown, Romeo Watkins, and later Rev. Brown's son, Melvin.

Mack's Nursery: Mack Nursery was opened in 1970. It was the first black-owned nursery in the area. The Macks lived on Ridgeway Street, and she had an addition added to the back of her house to start the nursery. Later, as it grew, she had a basement built and moved the nursery there. The nursery continued to grow, and they built the nursery next to Ridgewood Baptist church. This was a great achievement for the neighborhood. This was the first black nursery in the neighborhood. Many parents could go to work because they had somewhere reliable to care for their children. This was during the era when children had to attend a daycare program before starting school.

Hicks Nursery School: Hick's Nursery was opened in 1975. It was also black owned. The Hicks' lived on Woodbrier Street, next door to Ridgewood Elementary School. Hick's Nursery had several grade levels. It also had an after-school component added to it. I remember the first graduation I attended. My grandson, Quintus II, was one of the first graduates. To see the children march in their hats and gowns was a great first step for them. It was hoped that they would have many more graduations, and many of the children attending that nursery, as well as the other nursery, inspired them to go higher in education, and many of them have.

Trapp Electric: Trapp Electric was black-owned. Mr. Charles Trapp lived on Lawton Street, but his business was located on the 1500 block of Park Street. The building is still located there. Mr. Trapp was the first black electric journeyman in the state of South

Carolina. Mr. Nelson was the second black journeyman (as I was told by Mr. Trapp) had his own business also. Mr. Nelson also lived in the Ridgewood Community. We had many men pattern their lives after them and were successful. Mr. Mark Martin and Mr. Paul Darby were also electricians.

Hollis Construction Company: The Hollis brothers, who ran a black-owned business, lived in Ridgewood; one on Lawton Street and the other on Ridgeway Street. They did cement work. This trade was shared with many young men in the community, and it became a livelihood for them and their families. This also holds true for others, who patterned their lives after these men by starting their own businesses. There was much inspiration displayed and given to the young men in the community. It also opened up many job opportunities.

McRank's Cabinet Makers: McRank's, black-owned, was located on the corner of Eau Claire and Dixie Avenue. The McRanks lived on Summit Avenue. The building was a block long, and many of the men in the community worked there. They made cabinets of all styles. McRank later sold the property to a Piggy Wiggly chain.

Belin and Nye Meat Market is black and white-owned and located on the corner of Summit and Monticello. At one time, the entrance to the store was on Summit Ave. Today, the market's appearance has changed, and the entrance now faces Monticello Road. The market remains in the neighborhood today.

Martins Electric and Realtors: Black-owned. The Martins lived on Lewis and Ridgewood Camp Road. They had a Barber Shop on Monticello Road that was rented out; the building was torn down in 2019. They rented many houses in the community. The Martins also hired many men in the community to work.

The ABC Store: The smallest business in Ridgewood, which still remains on Monticello Road. This, maybe an eight-by-eight, building was owned by Mr. Mack Todley and later Mr. Leroy Moss. Mr. Moss was a blind man, and it was amazing to us children because, despite being blind, he had a business. We used to wonder how he knew how much change to give people. To my recollection, he was never robbed, and the men who went in there to buy liquor looked out for him. Sometimes, we would stop by to speak, and if a customer was in there, he would ask them, "How big is this bill?" They would tell him, and he would give them the correct change. He knew where all the items on the shelves were. Honesty was really important, and they knew not to cheat.

This was the smallest building in the neighborhood that was a liquor store owned by Mr. Moss, the blind man.

The Young's Drive Inn: Robert Lee and Estelle rented a building next to the ABC store on Monticello Road. The building was renovated, and they sold candy, food, and drinks. It was open because the children on Lawton Street, Ridgeway Street, and Knightner Street who rode the school bus had nowhere to go when it rained. We would open early in the morning so the children wouldn't have to stand out in the cold weather. In the afternoon, we would open it for the older people to come and socialize.

Educators: There were many school teachers in our community. Many of the teachers lived in the community. Many of them did not drive, so they would rent rooms from some of the families in the neighborhood and go home on the weekend. As time passed, schools were integrated, and the black schools lost their best teacher, and the black communities lost a lot of their strength. Children could no longer visit the teachers, and parents could no longer see the teachers on Sundays in church to talk with them. The school was torn down in the eighties. Today it is a park for the community, located on Woodbrier Street.

Preachers: There were many preachers in the community. Some had churches in the nearby community, and others had churches in rural areas.

Private Taxi Service: Growing up, we didn't know anything about taxi service. There were people in the community who had vehicles, but some of them would not give you a ride or take you anywhere. These were the families with vehicles: Rev. William McIlwain, Mr. Simon Reese, Mr. Louis Gates, Mr. Frank Lawhorn, Mr. Reuben Trapp, Mr. Charles Trapp, Mr. Bickley, Mr. Leroy Watkins, and Mr. Mark Martin. Rev. McIlwain and Mr. Reese would give you a ride without cost. When school was in, Rev. McIlwain and Mr. Reese would check the bus stops to see who missed the bus; they would make sure you were in school. They would carry you to school at C. A. Johnson and Booker T. Washington. If Mr. Reese gave you a ride from Eau Claire High School, when he got to Mr. Clark's store, he would put the car in neutral and coast down Monticello Road to save gas. Mr. Frank wouldn't carry you anywhere if you didn't have any money. The other men with cars would allow you to ride to other churches with them if there was a big meeting or some other program. Mr. Martin didn't ride anybody but his family.

Chapter 16

The Caddies and Golfers

The Ridgewood Community was blessed to have a large country club, The Ridgewood Country Club. The young men in the community would go there to caddy. When there was a Tournament, the men and women would make extra money working the tournament.

The Ridgewood Country Club was a renowned golf club, and famous golfers played there. As time passed, Mr. Willie Wise, from the neighborhood, got the owners to allow the guys who caddied to play golf on Sundays if nothing was going on. This was in the late fifties and sixties. From this, first, there were the men, and later, the women became interested in playing golf. From this, the Ridgewood Golf Club, the black group, was formed.

They participated in tournaments all over South Carolina, Georgia, and North Carolina. Some of the players from the community were James Trapp, William Trapp, James James, Howard Trapp, Thomas Wise, and Joseph Thompson. Romeo Watkins, Robert Lee Reed, David Bethel, James Walker, Johnny Geter, Robert Lee Young, Henry Walker, Louis Trapp, George Green,

John Edward Bethel, Leroy Williams Sr., Toney Cutner, John Cutner, Forest Tucker, Howard Taylor, Rev. James Taylor, John Washington, Curtis Martin, Tommy Martin, Arthur Gold, and Leroy" Buck" Watkins Jr. The men who were a part of the Ridgewood Golf Club were very good, and they surprised many black golfers in other areas where they played.

There was also a women's group. Mrs. Mattie Lee Williams and Ruth Reed are the ladies that I knew from the Ridgewood Community. As I recall, Mrs. Mattie L. Williams won many awards as a golfer.

Chapter 17

Moving ON

As time passed and our neighborhood grew, it was amazing how many of us learned different professions by watching others. To succeed, coming from a community that was called the ghetto, we have made great progress. I would be remiss if I didn't name some of the businesses that came from our community.

These are some of the businesses formed by the men and women of our neighborhood. Some of the successful people did not go to college but had a good business and lived very well. Some of them knew that their parents couldn't afford to send them to college, so they learned a trade from the older men and women in the community and kept it moving.

Businesses:
Watkins Barber Shop
Joseph Thompson/Specializing in Brick Work: "As Long as they make bricks, we'll lay them."
Louis Trapp Cement Finisher
Trapp Electric (Robert)
Johnson Grocery

Estelle Trapp Young

Hollis Construction Company
Joe's Barber Shop
Howard Trapp Cleaning Service
Young's Drive Inn
Mack Richardson One Stop Shop
Mack's Nursery
Hick's Nursery

Chapter 18

Community Icons

Mr. Benjamin Mack was a father, a brother, and a teacher. He was also a leader and an activist who worked for and with Dr. Martin Luther King, Jr. Mr. Charles Trapp was the first black electric journeyman in the state. As an activist, he worked with Dr. King and the Southern Christian Leadership Conference.

Mr. Nelson and Mr. Willie Martin, electricians. Mrs. Mamie L. Floyd, teacher and activist. The Eau Claire Post Office was renamed in her honor for her services to the community and state. Estelle Young was also an activist for civil rights and worked with Dr. Martin Luther King. She traveled throughout the state, teaching blacks how to read and write their names instead of making an X for their signature. She was the first female to integrate the Columbia Police Department administration office. The first black female to be promoted to the ranks of Corporal and Sergeant. The first female ever in the history of the Columbia Police Department was promoted to the rank of Inspector and Captain.

There are many teachers and PhDs in the

community, musicians, lawyers, preachers, nurses, and police officers. Mr. C. Pearson and Mr. Eleazer were the first police officers in the community to work for the Columbia Police Department.

Armed forces, Larry Knightner, Major General (Two Star), Retired Federal Civilian as the South Carolina State Director of the United States Department of Housing and Urban Development (HUD), NFL Player Robert Taylor, Glenis Pearson, Grant Writer, helped many communities, as a grant writer, be redeveloped. Construction workers who taught so many of the young men in the community how to lay bricks, pour cement, and many other trades. Most importantly, it is about good work ethics.

About The Author

Estelle Trapp Young was born in Columbia, South Carolina. She was raised in Ridgewood, a product of Lawton Street; she attended Ridgewood Elementary School. A graduate of C.A. Johnson High, Estelle received her Apprentice and Certified license as a Cosmetologist.

She was employed by the City of Columbia Police Department as a meter maid and, later, the first black to work in administration. She later joined the police force. She surely was a Trailblazer. She was the first Black female Corporal and Sergeant on the force and the first female Inspector and Captain in the department's history.

She received her Associate of Science in Criminal Justice and Bachelor of Arts in Interdisciplinary Studies from the University of South Carolina. She received her Master of Arts in Human Resource Development from Webster University and is a graduate of South Carolina Criminal Justice Academy. She also earned certificates in various disciplines from Midland Technical College, Columbia, SC. She has also earned many certificates from Midland Technical College, Columbia, SC.

Mrs. Young received many awards, certificates, and recognition for her work from organizations, schools, churches, and community groups. A few of them include the Martin Luther King Drum Major for Justice, the United Capital State Police Dignitary Protection Division, the Service to Mankind Award, the Richland Sertoma Club, and the District Award for Service to Mankind Award.

Mrs. Young also received Resolutions from the General Assembly of South Carolina and the City of Columbia. She was a nominee of the South Carolina Law Enforcement Association - International Chief of Police.

Other honors include Advisor of the Year from the SC Scales Explorer Program and the South Carolina Association of Law Enforcement, recognition from the North Columbia Business Association, the Eau Clara Community Council, and the North Region Community Response Team.

International Police Exchange Programme Between Columbia South Carolina Police Department and the Trinidad and Tobago Police Service, POLICIA DE PUERTO RICO PROTECCION INTEGRIDAD AWARD, the Whitney M. Young Jr. Service Award, Woman of the Year - Midland's Chapter of America Business Women's Association (ABWA), Business Associate of the Year - Midland Chapter (ABWA), the

Jean Hopkins Service Award, Women of Distinction Girl Scouts of South Carolina Mountains to Midlands Award.

She also received the Leadership Summit, powered by IMARA Women Magazine Trailblazer Leadership Award, the Dedicated Service Award - KOBAN Columbia, the Ridgewood Baptist Church Woman of the Year Award, and other awards for dedicated church service.

She has traveled to many foreign places, the Holy Land, which included Bethlehem, Jerusalem, and the Jordan River. Rome, the Sicilian island of Syracuse, France, the Neverlands, the Battle of the Bulge Site (between Belgium and Luxembourg), the Leaning Tower of Pisa in Pisa, Italy, Dubai in the United Arab Emirates, Germany, Japan, India, Amsterdam, Brussels, Africa, and many islands such as St. Maarten, St. Kitts, St. Croix, Curaçao, Palladium, Mexico, Cabo San Lucas, Jamacia, Aruba, Belize, the Cayman Islands, and many other historical sites.

Estelle has several mottos/quotes she has shared over the years: "Don't Look Down on a Man unless you're picking him up with God's help." Anonymous.

This one is a paraphrase from Mahalia Jackson, the famous singer, "If I can help somebody as I travel along, then my living shall not be in vain.".

Her favorite scripture is Psalms 37.

Made in the USA
Columbia, SC
27 May 2025